MARGARET THATCHER: THE IRON LADY WHO MADE HISTORY

BIOGRAPHY 3RD GRADE

CHILDREN'S BIOGRAPHY BOOKS

Speedy Publishing LLC

40 E. Main St. #1156

Newark, DE 19711

www.speedypublishing.com

Copyright 2017

In this book, we're going to talk about the life of Margaret Thatcher. So, let's get right to it!

MARGARET THATCHER

WHO WAS MARGARET THATCHER?

From 1979 to 1990, Margaret Thatcher was the United Kingdom's Prime Minister. This position is the most important political position in Great Britain and she was the first woman to hold that position. She had very conservative political views.

A conservative is a person who has traditional views. During the Cold War with the Soviet Union, she defended democracy and was an important leader and ally for the United States.

MAP OF SOVIET UNION IN SOVIET UNION FLAG COLORS

MARGARET THATCHER'S EARLY LIFE

Margaret was born in the city of Grantham, England in 1925. Her father was a small business owner who had a local grocery store. Margaret had an older sister named Muriel and their family lived upstairs from the store.

BIRTHPLACE OF MARGARET THATCHER

GRANTHAM, LINCOLNSHIRE, ENGLAND

Margaret's father held a position as alderman, which is an elected member of the City Council, in the city of Grantham and for a time he was mayor. Her father's positions helped Margaret to learn about politics.

At the beginning, Margaret didn't think about a career in politics. She was an excellent student and was accepted at Oxford University. She graduated from Oxford with a Chemistry degree.

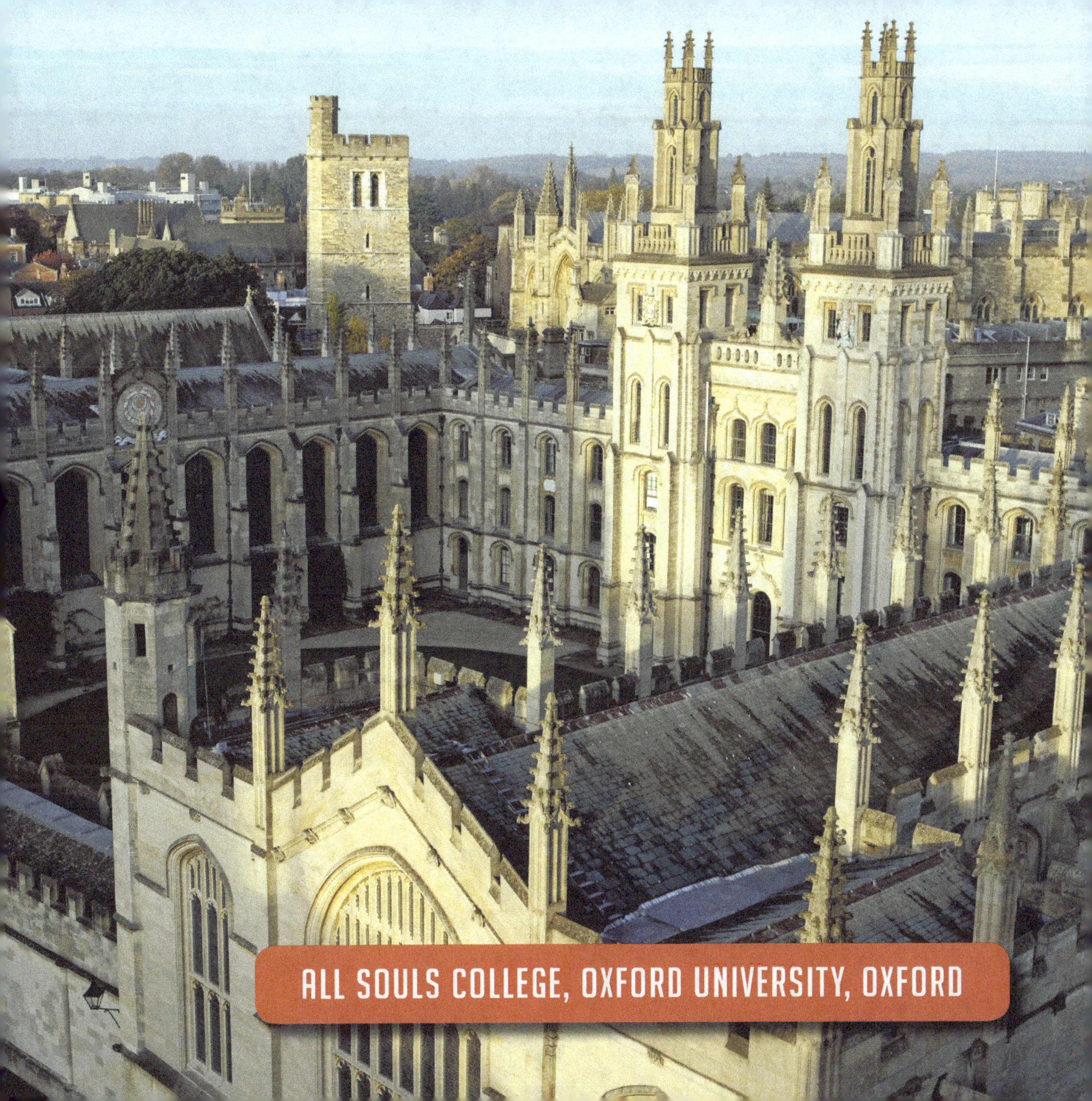
ALL SOULS COLLEGE, OXFORD UNIVERSITY, OXFORD

CHEMIST ANALYZING LIQUIDS IN LABORATORY

While she was at Oxford, Margaret developed more of an interest in politics. She gained a strong belief that she held the rest of her life. She believed that government should not intervene in business. In other words, the government shouldn't place a lot of regulations on businesses. While at Oxford, she was president of the University's Conservative Association. When she graduated in 1947 at the age of 22, she applied for and got a job working as a chemist.

POLITICAL BEGINNINGS

After several years, Margaret decided that she wanted to try and run for office. She tried to obtain a seat in parliament in Dartford two separate times, but she lost on both occasions. This area of Britain isn't conservative so it wasn't likely that she would be able to obtain the position.

THE QUEEN ELIZABETH BRIDGE IN DARTFORD, KENT, ENGLAND

THATCHERS AND BUSHES AT CHEQUERS

Two months after her second loss, she married Denis Thatcher, a very successful businessman. Their marriage lasted 50 years.

The experience losing the seat was ultimately good for her and prompted her to go back to the university in 1952.

This time she took classes to earn a degree in law, which would be helpful to her future political career. She and her husband had twins, a boy and a girl, the following year. In 1953, after completing her law degree, Thatcher became a barrister, which is a type of lawyer.

BARRISTER IN COURT HOLDING BRIEF AND BOOK

THE PALACE OF WESTMINSTER IS THE MEETING PLACE
OF THE HOUSE OF COMMONS

She didn't stay out of politics for too long. In 1959, she obtained a seat in the House of Commons, as a representative for Finchley, an area of north London. At this time, her political career started to move more rapidly. In 1961, she was appointed the position of under secretary in the parliament with the responsibility of pensions as well as national insurance.

When the Labour Party, the party that was the other political group in Great Britain, took government control, she became part of what is known as the "Shadow Cabinet." This is a group of leaders who would be part of the Cabinet if their party were in power.

GIRLS DRINKING FREE MILK AT SCHOOL

CONSERVATIVES RETURN TO POWER

By 1970, the Labour Party was out of power and Margaret's party, the Conservative party, had taken control of parliament. Margaret was appointed to a Secretary of State position. Her responsibility was education as well as science. She did away with free milk in school, and she was taunted with "Thatcher, Thatcher, Milk Snatcher."

She was frustrated not just because of the bad press she was getting, but because she couldn't get Edward Heath, the Prime Minister at the time, to take her ideas seriously. She became discouraged that women would never be allowed into the world of politics in Great Britain. In fact, during a television appearance that she made in 1973, she was quoted as saying there wouldn't be a woman in the position of Prime Minister during her lifetime. Little did she know that she would soon prove that statement wrong herself!

EDWARD HEATH

Margaret continued to rise in influence within her party. In 1974, the Conservatives lost control of parliament to the Labour party again. During this time, Margaret gained in power within her party. In 1975, Margaret took over the leadership position in the Conservative party, beating out the former Prime Minister, Edward Heath. It was the first time a woman had ever been in the position as "Leader of the Opposition."

At this time, Great Britain was in chaos. The government was close to being bankrupt and the citizens were very unhappy because so many people were unemployed. There were many conflicts happening with labor unions as well. Because of all this unrest, the Conservatives were able to gain power and the Labour Party lost the majority vote.

Margaret Thatcher made history in 1979 when as the leader of the Conservative party she was appointed to be Britain's Prime Minister, the first woman Prime Minister in the history of the country. She was fifty-four years old and beginning over a decade of service to the country she loved as Prime Minister.

IN MEMORY OF
THOSE WHO
LIBERATED US

14 JUNE 1982

FALKLANDS WAR MEMORIAL

POSITION AS PRIME MINISTER

There were many crucial events and prestigious accomplishments during the decade that Margaret Thatcher held her position. Here are some of the most important:

WAR ON THE FALKLAND ISLANDS

Three years after Margaret became Prime Minister, the Falkland Islands, which were under British control, were invaded by Argentina.

Thatcher didn't hesitate. She sent British troops to take back control of the islands. The battle wasn't easy, but the armed forces fought back and were able to regain control of the islands a few months later.

ABANDONED CANON FALKLAND ISLANDS

UNITED STATES PRESIDENT RONALD REAGAN

THE COLD WAR

Thatcher played a very important part in the end of the Cold War. She worked with United States President Ronald Reagan to oppose communism in the Soviet Union and elsewhere in the world.

In fact, it was the Russians who gave her the nickname "The Iron Lady." Yuri Gavrilov, a Soviet captain, coined the phrase for her because of her ironclad opposition to communism.

TWO IRON LADIES - GOLDA MEIR AND MARGARET THATCHER

MIKHAIL GORBACHEV

Despite this, she was open to working with President Reagan and Soviet leader, Mikhail Gorbachev, to achieve a peaceful cooperation between the Soviet Union, Great Britain, and the United States. The joint alliance of Great Britain and the United States helped to end the Cold War during her time in office.

UNION REFORMS

One of the goals that Margaret wanted to achieve was to make the trade unions less powerful. When miners went on strike and used the trade unions to make their demands, she stood her ground. Eventually, due to her actions the strikes minimized in numbers and the number of days lost on the job were reduced benefitting the businesses and ultimately benefitting the workers as well.

MINER IN THE WORKPLACE

RONALD REAGAN AND MARGARET THATCHER

CHANGING INDUSTRIES TO PRIVATE INSTEAD OF GOVERNMENT CONTROL

Thatcher and Reagan both believed that the government should give up some controls and allow private industry to take their place in certain cases. She thought that if utility services were run by private companies it would help the economy in Britain. It took some time, but eventually the utilities and some of the other government-run industries were converted to private companies. Prices came down, which was helpful for Britain's citizens.

ECONOMIC REFORMS

At the start of Thatcher's term in office she implemented a number of changes that weren't popular at the time, but eventually resulted in a stronger economy. She privatized certain industries, worked to reform the unions, and made changes in the tax structure. She also increased the rates of interest. It took a few years, but the economy, which had been in a state of chaos when she took office, began to improve.

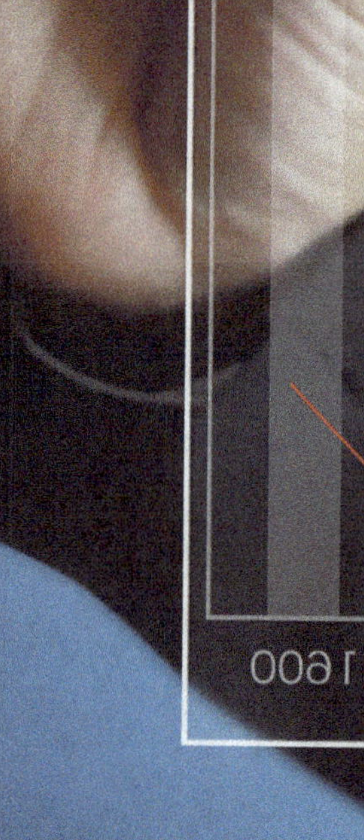

BRIGHTON HOTEL BOMBING

ATTEMPT ON THATCHER'S LIFE

In 1984, Margaret's life was threatened when the Irish Republican Army attempted to assassinate her. They set off a bomb at the hotel where she was staying. The bomb damaged her room, but luckily she survived. Five people were killed and thirty-one people were injured. Thatcher was scheduled to speak at a conference the following morning and she gave her speech as planned. Her cool-headed response to the act of terrorism won her admiration around the world.

LIFE AFTER POLITICAL OFFICE

In 1990, Margaret resigned from the position of Prime Minister under pressure from her party. Party members were concerned that her tax policies were going to be unpopular and hurt the Conservatives in the elections.

MARGARET THATCHER AT KENNEDY SPACE CENTER

RONALD REAGAN'S FUNERAL

Despite this, Thatcher continued to serve as a parliament member until 1992 when she formally retired. She wrote quite a few books and made presentations and speeches for the next decade. Around 2002 her health began to fail and she suffered a series of strokes. She was grief-stricken when her husband passed away in 2003 and the following year she suffered another personal blow when her strong ally Ronald Reagan passed away.

She passed away at the age of 87 in 2013, an iron lady until the end. A sculpture in her memory stands tall and proud in the House of Commons in Parliament.

MARGARET THATCHER COFFIN AT ST. PAULS

Now you know more about the life of Margaret Thatcher. You can find more Biography books from Baby Professor by searching the website of your favorite book retailer.

Visit
BABY PROFESSOR
EDUCATION KIDS
www.BabyProfessorBooks.com
to download Free Baby Professor eBooks and view
our catalog of new and exciting Children's Books